Earned Value Management

APM Guidelines

Earned Value Management

APM Guidelines

Association for Project Management

Association for Project Management
Ibis House, Regent Park
Summerleys Road, Princes Risborough
Buckinghamshire
HP27 9LE

First edition 2002
Revised with minor corrections 2008

British Library Cataloguing in Publication Data is available
ISBN 10: 1-903494-26-5
ISBN 13: 978-1-903494-26-4

Cover design by Mark Design
Typeset by RefineCatch Limited
Copy editor: Merle Read
Publishing Manager: Ingmar Folkmans

Contents

Figures and tables

Foreword

The first edition of this guideline was published in 2002. It was well received both nationally and internationally.

In late 2007 the guideline was reviewed and overhauled. Particular thanks are due to Jim Malkin for overseeing the final draft through to its publication.

This revision aimed to fix errors identified over the years and to improve clarity. It is still reciprocal with the American ANSI 748 Earned Value Standard.

This guide will be formally reviewed again in 2011. Please address any comments and feedback to the Chairman of the APM Earned Value Management Specific Interest Group at www.apm.org.uk.

Steve Wake
Chairman APM Earned Value Management
Specific Interest Group

1
Introduction

Earned value management is a project control process based on a strutured approach to planning, cost collection and performance measurement. It facilitates the integration of project scope, time and cost objectives and the establishment of a baseline plan for performance measurement (Association for Project Management, 2006).

The establishment of a performance measurement baseline (PMB) is essential to conducting successful EVM and consists of:

- defined scope and assumptions;
- activities scheduled in logical sequence;
- resources/costs (labour and materials).

We need to know:

- what the plan is;
- what the project has achieved;
- what has been spent to date.

Earned value helps us manage by:

- providing data to enable objective measurement of project status;
- providing a basis for estimating final cost;
- predicting when the project will be complete;
- supporting the effective management of resources;
- providing a means of managing and controlling change.

Informed and effective decision making is enabled by knowing:

- what has been achieved of the plan;
- what it has cost to achieve the planned work;
- if the work achieved is costing more or less than was planned;
- if the project is ahead of or behind the planned schedule.

Good planning leads to good project execution and good management information. Poor planning can lead to poor execution and poor EVM information. The plan must be maintained in accordance with authorised project changes. EVM will accurately show deviations from the plan, but it may not be immediately evident that a flawed plan is being tracked.

2
Applicability

Earned Value Management: APM Guidelines can be applied to projects of varying size, scope and duration to ensure that the EVM process is operated in a consistent manner across all implementing teams. Each implementing project should take into account:

- project specific requirements;
- customer requirements;
- lessons learnt from previous projects;
- IT toolset requirements;
- impact on resources and infrastructure.

Project managers should ensure that progress and performance measurements are realistic and are in accordance with this guide.

3

Basic requirements for an earned value system

This document is a guide to the process for implementing and running an earned value management system. The following list describes the fundamental steps of the process that should be undertaken:

* define the scope (section 5.1.1);
* use a work breakdown structure (WBS) to define the work (section 5.1.2.2);
* establish organisational responsibility for work accomplishment in an organisation breakdown structure (OBS) (section 5.1.2.3);
* ensure management subsystems support each other, the WBS and the OBS (section 5.1.2.4);
* distribute the budget into the WBS (section 5.2.4);
* schedule all authorised work using a logic-linked method (section 5.2.2);
* identify a method of measuring achievement (section 5.2.5);
* spread the budget over time consistent with the schedule for the work (section 5.2.6);
* baseline the plan (section 5.2.6);
* record direct and indirect costs (section 5.3.1);
* collect and analyse performance data at the control account level on a periodic basis (section 5.4.2);
* produce forecasts for remaining work (section 5.4.3);
* incorporate all authorised changes in a timely and controlled manner (section 5.5).

4

What is earned value management?

4.1 EARNED VALUE MANAGEMENT PRINCIPLES

EVM is about establishing and managing goals throughout the life of a project. It comprises the following:

* definition and authorisation of the contract scope of work;
* development of a 'baseline' against which cost, schedule and technical performance can be measured;
* objective performance measurement;
* variance analysis and corrective action reporting;
* disciplined and timely incorporation of 'baseline' changes.

An earned value management system (EVMS) will provide the following:

* verifiable status reports;
* clear objective analysis;
* considered reasoning;
* accountability in the decision-making process;
* awareness of impact on the schedule and cost across the project;
* visibility of results.

A system should be created that will enable the measurement of the four key data elements essential to EVMS, namely:

1. The budgeted cost of work scheduled (BCWS) or planned value (PV) – i.e. what we are going to do, the plan: the schedule for the expenditure of budgeted resources as necessary to meet project scope and schedule objectives. It is important to understand that BCWS is a *schedule*, stated in the value of work to be performed, and is therefore a basis for both time and cost assessment of the progress on a project.
2. The actual cost of work performed (ACWP) or actual cost (AC) – i.e. what the work achieved actually cost.
3. The budgeted cost of work performed (BCWP) or earned value (EV) – i.e. what the amount of work achieved should have cost, according to the planned budget: the *earned value* for the work actually achieved.

5

4. The estimate at completion (EAC) of the project. This is the ACWP to date, plus the most knowledgeable estimate of remaining requirements, scope, schedule and cost.

Guidelines exist for companies to use in establishing and applying an EVMS. These guidelines are expressed in fundamental terms and provide flexibility for each company to optimise its system, and be fully accountable for the effectiveness of its usage. These guidelines (or criteria) are recognised as an international standard, and are attached at Appendix A. An EVMS that is developed to meet the intent of the criteria, will allow key stakeholders, notably customers and shareholders, to gain confidence that projects are being managed and resources deployed in an effective and consistent manner against a recognised standard.

4.2 WHAT ARE THE BENEFITS?

Figure 4.1 shows the traditional budget vs. actual graph. It is traditionally used to compare budget with actual spend.

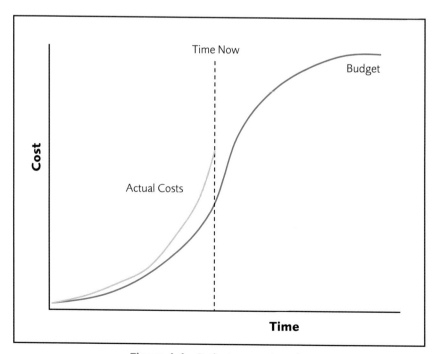

Figure 4.1 – Budget vs actual graph

The graph does *not* show:

- if the project is ahead of or behind schedule;
- if the project is truly over- or underspending;
- if the project is getting value for money;
- if money has been spent on the right things;
- if the problems are over or have only just begun.

The graph shown in Figure 4.2 is similar to the previous graph except that a measure of performance (or status value) has been included. The line included is the *earned value* or *achievement* line. This additional line represents the proportion of the budget that has actually been achieved.

  Figure 4.2 indicates the following additional information:

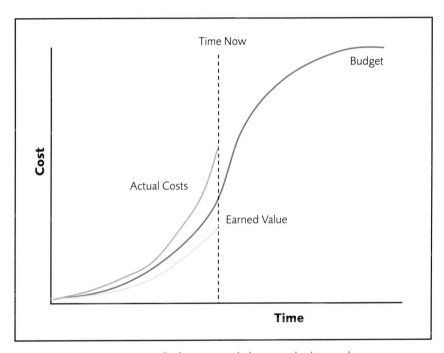

Figure 4.2 – Budget vs actual plus earned value graph

- the project is underachieving because the amount (value) of work completed (earned value) is less than that scheduled;
- the project is overspent because the cost of the work completed is greater that the budgeted cost of work completed (earned value);
- the cost performance is actually worse than was indicated on the traditional chart because it shows an over-expenditure coupled with underachievement of planned work scope;
- the project is spending money inefficiently, as it is costing more to achieve progress than planned. The cost problems do not appear to be contained, since the slope of the actual cost line is greater that the budgeted cost line; this indicates that the overspend is going to increase, even though the earned value line does look like it will intersect the budget cost line some time in the future. While schedule recovery may yet be possible, the cost impact is unlikely to be recovered.

4.3 USING PERFORMANCE MEASUREMENTS

Any measurements of performance are **indicators** of the efficiency or perform-ance of a project. As such, they should be used as **one** of the many criteria on which project managers should base their decisions, having interpreted the information and placed it in context.

Performance measurements indicate where shortfalls are occurring or likely to occur. These can be used to identify where extra resources, management actions or other support are required in order to overcome problems. They are early indicators of problems and give pointers as to what might happen to the project if actions are not taken.

5
Process discussion

Earned value management may be considered as a number of management processes, as follows:

- definition;
- planning;
- data collection;
- analysis, review and action;
- change management;
- risk management.

The following sections provide guidelines as to the main elements contained within each process. At the end of each process, a checklist of key activities is provided.

5.1 DEFINITION

Organising the work and resources to achieve the requirements of the project. The *definition* process is principally concerned with defining the work to be done – as a WBS – and assigning that work to specific parts of the project's organisation via the OBS. The WBS and OBS should be aligned and combined to produce a responsibility assignment matrix (RAM).

5.1.1 Project scope/statement of work (SOW)

A SOW can define the project scope to include the overall requirements, including deliverables, for the project. It forms the basis for allocating work, budget and schedule requirements.

The extent to which the SOW fully describes the requirements of the project will have an impact on the ability of the EVM system to provide objective measures of performance against the original project requirement.

5.1.2 Project breakdown structures

5.1.2.1 Why have structures?

Breakdown structures are essential to project management in the following areas:

9

- the definition and clarification of the work to be performed;
- the assignment of tasks to organisations responsible for carrying out the work;
- thorough planning;
- the establishment and control of baselines;
- the objective measurement of achievement against the plan at levels where the work is being performed;
- the collection, summarising and reporting to higher management, and the customer, for use in the decision-making process;
- performance measurements.

Before work assignments are made and the associated operating budgets are established, a project should establish a WBS and an OBS, and integrate the two into a responsibility assignment matrix (see Figure 5.1 below). All control accounts should be identified (see section 5.1.2.4). These steps are necessary before any measurements of performance can be undertaken.

5.1.2.2   Work breakdown structure

The hierarchical subdivision of a project into discrete elements of work is known as a WBS. The WBS is developed by identifying high-level elements of work necessary to meet the project requirements. These major elements are then broken down into smaller components. This breakdown continues until the lowest level of detail deemed necessary for management visibility and control is established. All aspects of the contract are included and the WBS can be viewed as a graphical hierarchical representation of the SOW.

When developing a WBS, it is advisable to concentrate solely on the work content of the project.

Projects may choose to use a work breakdown structure dictionary (WBSD). The purpose of the dictionary is to describe the entire scope of work to be undertaken by the project. It must capture the contract scope and all contract requirements. To enable this to be checked it must provide a ready reference between the WBS and contract elements. It also provides the basis for the statement of work included on the control account Plans.

For each element of the WBS, the dictionary should contain:

- a contract number;
- a WBS number and title;
- the WBSD issue number and date;
- the contract paragraph number;
- a statement of work including all contract deliverables to be produced as part of the work element;

The WBS dictionary should include all elements to be subcontracted and should specifically identify the subcontractor undertaking the WBS element.

5.1.2.3 Organisation breakdown structure

Projects usually involve people from a variety of functions and departments across a company. A fundamental requirement of a well-managed project is a clear people organisation. Where matrix management structures are used, this clarity in organisational definition is particularly important.

In order to clarify and define the organisation, an organisation chart or organisation breakdown structure should be developed. Roles, responsibilities and accountabilities should be clearly defined for all staff and communicated across the project team. Staff being introduced into the project should have a clear knowledge of whom they report to and for what work they are responsible.

Loose definition of roles, responsibilities authorities and accountabilities will lead to ambiguities and confusion in the management of the project.

5.1.2.4 Control accounts

An OBS reflects the way in which the project has organised the people who will achieve the work. A WBS reflects the way in which work has been subdivided.

To assign work responsibilities to appropriate organisational elements the WBS must be interrelated with the OBS. The assignment of lower-level work breakdown elements to responsible organisations provides a key control point for management purposes and cost collection.

The integration of the WBS and the OBS at the control account level can be displayed as a matrix, with the OBS elements listed on one axis and the WBS elements on the other. This is the responsibility assignment matrix, where each element is a control account (CA) with a control account manager (CAM) responsible for its completion to budget.

A control account will normally comprise a number of work packages (WPs). In some cases, a control account may be a single work package. Each work package should have the following attributes:

- defined scope of work;
- measure of achievement;
- traceability up through the WBS;
- budget;
- assignment of responsibility;
- start and finish dates.

If it is not possible to define a work package to the detail noted above, then it should be identified as a planning package within the control account – see section 5.2.1.

11

Once the WBS (and the dictionary, if used) has been completed, it should be reconciled back to the requirement and other formal agreements to ensure that all aspects of the project have been included.

It is important that the control account is identified for each work area. The control account is the main action point for the planning and control of project work. It is the point where management responsibility for the individual control accounts is assigned. A manager may be responsible for many control accounts, but a control account may have only one manager.

The control account in an integrated management system is the lowest level in the structure at which comparisons between actual costs and budgeted costs are normally required by management. However, analysis will also be done at lower levels, as required for local control. Most management actions taken at higher levels are triggered by significant problems identified at the control account level. For this reason, the levels selected for the establishment of the organisation and the control accounts should be carefully considered at the outset of the project.

The RAM (Figure 5.1) shows the level of control that has been established. If the accounts identified are too big or too small, too many or too few, they should be reconsidered and changed accordingly.

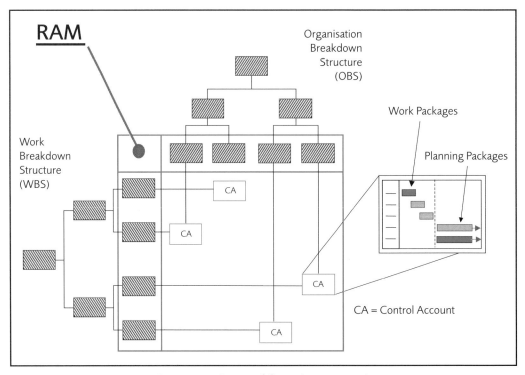

Figure 5.1 – Responsibility assignment matrix

The following aspects of the project come together at the control account:

- budgets;
- schedules;
- forecasts;
- work assignments;
- cost collection;
- progress assessment;
- problem identification;
- corrective actions.

5.1.2.5 Subcontract management

It is appropriate to reflect the requirements of *Earned Value Management: APM Guidelines* in any subcontract. Reporting requirements should be consistent with project risk, size, complexity and other factors.

Processes should be in place to ensure that subcontractor's plans are represented within the project plans/schedules in order to derive a view of total project performance. Plans derived for a project can be very large and complex, and so decisions have to be taken as to the level of detail to be incorporated into the plans. If there is too much detail, the maintenance of the plan becomes a burdensome overhead, while if there is insufficient detail, the exact status of the project is difficult to ascertain.

5.1.3   Key activities in definition

1. Review the project requirements and establish key deliverables.
2. Develop a WBS.
3. Develop an OBS.
4. Generate a RAM identifying control accounts.
5. Produce WBSD statements for each WBS element down to the lowest appropriate level (e.g. work packages and planning packages).
6. Determine and agree requirements for flowdown of EVM requirements into subcontracts.

5.2   PLANNING

What needs to be done, by whom and by when? The *planning* processes are primarily concerned with establishing a baseline for performance measurement that encompasses the following:

- a plan of logically scheduled activities that reflect the project objectives, goals and milestones;

- budgets/resources agreed and assigned to these activities;
- objective achievement measures defined.

These will constitute the project baseline against which the project will be monitored and controlled throughout its life cycle, and will allow the achievement of project and business success criteria.

5.2.1 Work packages, planning packages and activities

The work package is the lowest level at which performance data is normally analysed. It is therefore important to balance the length and scope of the work package against reporting cycle lengths, and to consider when and how to earn 'value'. Each work package must have a clearly defined start condition and finish point, with all deliverables defined. The scope of each work package must be unambiguously defined with the procedures to be followed identified.
  Each work package comprises a number of activities to be performed. Each activity can be assigned to only a single work package. Each activity is a stepping stone towards completion of its parent work package. Figure 5.2 shows a schematic of the relationship between work packages, planning packages and activities. The activity is where duration, resources and costs are estimated; dependencies are shown between activities.

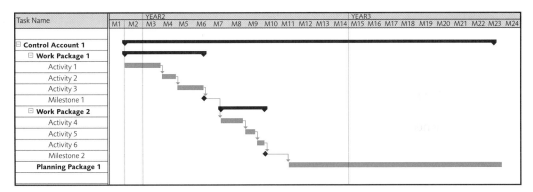

Figure 5.2 – Relationship between control account, work package, and activity.

Planning packages (PPs) represent work that cannot yet be planned as work packages because of a lack of detailed information. Normally this is future work that is not scheduled to be started for at least three full months from the current date. Work in the near future that cannot be planned in work packages may indicate a problem of work definition.

PPs are structured below the control account level, have a defined scope of work and are allocated a time-phased budget. They have scheduled start and finish dates (hence a duration) and a defined budget and scope.

Planning packages must be converted into work packages before work can commence upon them, i.e. before they can 'earn' achievement, or have costs booked against them. The budget is withdrawn from the planning package and is used to establish work packages as their start date nears and the details of the tasks become clearer. The resulting work packages will contain the detailed activities, logic, milestones, resources and achievement measures.

The requirement for a periodic conversion, from planning package to work package, is the result of setting up the project using rolling wave planning, whereby only the current phase of a project is planned in detail and future phases are planned in outline. The conversion process is a fundamental aspect of project control using EVM and results in a more controlled project baseline.

5.2.2   Schedules

Scheduling is the process of determining when project activities will take place depending on defined durations and preceding activities. Schedule logic specifies when an activity should start or end on the basis of duration, predecessors, external predecessor relationships, resource availability or target dates. For a definition of a schedule see Appendix B.

Schedules can be created to reflect various elements of the WBS, from the highest-level plan to detailed work package schedules containing the lowest level of activity. These schedules form the basis for assessing actual progress and comparing actual cost against work performed.

All contractual milestones should be included within the schedule from the start of the project. These contractual milestones should be logically linked to appropriate activities so that any changes to forecast dates are applied throughout the schedule.

It is essential in any EVMS that activities on the current critical path are identified. This will enable variances from the plan to be appropriately categorised – e.g. 'late but float remains' as opposed to 'late and on critical path'. To preclude excessive workload on large projects, a project may choose to exclude the lower-levels of schedules from the network used for critical path analyses. However, the lower level schedules must always support the summary-level schedule so that all analyses have the same basis.

The overall scheduling process permits the integrated planning of project resources with the cost and schedule objectives of the project, and provides a means of measuring progress against planned effort. Scheduling and work scope definition are prerequisites for basic project management and effective cost control.

The baseline should respect all key milestones: the agreed contractual delivery milestones and appropriate internal indicator milestones. The key milestones should be used for measurement and control.

Schedules provide the time frame for activities to be performed and resources to be utilised.

Although each project has individual requirements, it is common practice for the project to be supported by a single schedule data set consisting of a series of detailed schedules built into an integrated network. This data set covers all work necessary to meet the requirements of the project. The schedule can be summarised to different levels of detail to accommodate the various levels of visibility and selection criteria required (Figure 5.3).

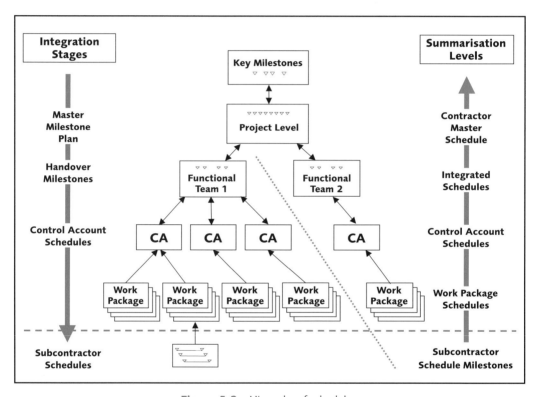

Figure 5.3 – Hierarchy of schedules

5.2.3   Subcontractor and schedule baseline relationship

The supplier's plans should detail an appropriate number of activities/ milestones required to effectively track and manage progress. These activities will be shown in the project schedule as either work packages/planning packages or as individual control accounts, depending on the level of detail to be reported. Whatever the level of incorporation, sufficient detail to provide visibility of actual status and early warning of potential problems and issues is vital. It is also important to structure the control accounts/work packages to enable the recording of both 'in-house' supplier management effort and specific subcontractor effort.

The resourcing/budgeting of the work should reflect the value of the item or service – as agreed in the contract – to allow a realistic expenditure profile or budget curve to be generated. Furthermore, there should be a discrete 'milestone' identified in every reporting period to allow the measurement of achievement on a regular basis. However, the supplier should be expected to provide a monthly progress report (or equivalent), irrespective of the detail of their schedule contained within the project schedule. This report can be used as the basis for claiming achievement (or otherwise).

The way in which subcontractor effort is integrated into the baseline (Figure 5.4) will differ according to their importance to the project. The distinction between major and minor subcontractor should be based upon factors such as equipment value, criticality (risk) to the project (e.g. single source supply) and/or whether they are an 'off the shelf' supplier.

Ideally, major subcontractors should be structured as single control accounts, not only because of their relative importance but also to provide the ability to clearly monitor their overall status.

Minor subcontractors should be structured within single work packages/PPs, with a control account conceivably containing several minor subcontractors. This still allows for appropriate visibility of performance, but not at the lower levels within the integrated baseline.

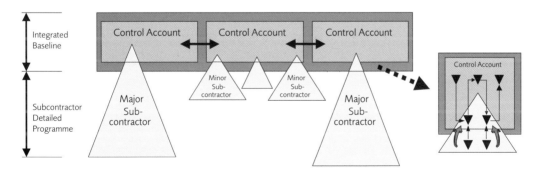

Figure 5.4 – Integration of subcontract effort

5.2.4 Setting budgets

Budgeting is the process of distributing or allocating cost targets to individual segments of work. Strict budget element relationships must exist at all times in order to ensure that the sum of the parts is equal to the whole. The hierarchy of budget elements is shown in Figure 5.5. This illustrates how the intermediate summations are defined leading to the contract budget baseline.

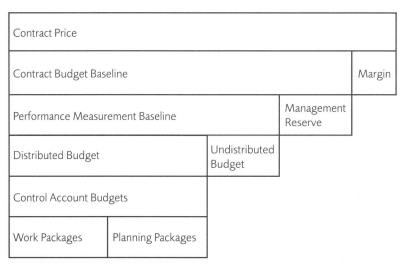

Figure 5.5 – Budget elements

5.2.4.1 Budget versus funds

Within an EVM system the concept of budgets is different from the concept of funds. While a budget represents the cost performance target for a specific effort, funds represent the money available for expenditure in the accomplishment of the effort. Budgets are established for the relevant elements of the work breakdown structure and are time-phased.

Budget cannot be spent; it is the funds that are consumed. Funds are authorised by the customer or by the company on a total or periodic basis.

The formulation of estimates at completion (EACs) provides the project with visibility of the anticipated/out turn funds required by forecasting the actual funding requirements for any approved statement of work element.

5.2.4.2 Budget cost types and rates

Projects usually involve many different types of costs that need to be summarised through various levels of detail. As work packages are subdivisions of work, then each work package will comprise a number of differing types of costs. Separate work packages should not be raised for different cost types. Within earned value management systems, specific terms are used to denote types of budgets, and each area of the budget has specific inclusions/exclusions.

Budgets (in terms of pounds, hours or other measurable units) should be allocated to every work package within each control account. Budgets should separately identify labour, material, subcontract and any other direct costs (see *distributed budget*, section 5.2.4.7).

It is the summation of all budgeted work that forms the performance measurement baseline.

5.2.4.3 Contract budget baseline

The contract budget baseline (CBB) is the total contract value minus the margin. The CBB represents the total budget of all authorised work for the contract comprising the management reserve (MR) and PMB. This should equal the sum of the authorised budgets.

Generally, the CBB is fixed throughout the duration of the project, unless amended through contractual change.

Project baseline budgeting activity results in the further dissection of the CBB with a PMB and a management reserve.

5.2.4.4 Management reserve

MR is a portion of the CBB. It is held separately for future allocation to control accounts and will be used, if required, to cover increased work-scope requirements due to any unforeseen changes that fall within the overall scope of the contract.

Management reserve must never be used to eliminate past or current cost or schedule variances. This does not preclude allocation of reserve to future efforts in problem areas if the project manager agrees there is due cause.

Management reserve should not be used for changes in work scope originating from the customer. These are covered by contract amendments with agreed prices. The CBB is then increased to reflect the changes in work scope and budget.

5.2.4.5 Performance measurement baseline

The PMB is the time-phased budget plan, representing all budgets against which the contract performance (cost and schedule) is measured, spread across the planned duration of the project. It is equal to the total allocated budget less management reserve, and is represented as the BCWS. The PMB consists of undistributed budget (UB) and distributed budget (DB):

$$PMB = UB + DB$$

19

5.2.4.6 Undistributed Budget

UB is an amount within the PMB which is identified to a defined scope of work, but which has not yet been allocated to control accounts. As work is defined and assigned to control accounts, the UB should be reduced accordingly.

Undistributed Budget is allocated primarily to accommodate temporary situations until control accounts can be agreed, or where contract requirements can be defined only in very general terms.

Procedures should be in place to ensure that UB set aside for specific but unallocated work is not distributed elsewhere.

5.2.4.7 Distributed budget

Distributed budget is allocated to control accounts and will form the majority of budgets within the PMB.

5.2.4.8 Funding issues

The difference between funds and budget has been described above (section 5.2.4.1). Funding represents the money available from the company or the customer, and as such is subject to external commercial constraints.

Changes to projected funding may include:

- amount available;
- time-phasing of funding availability.

In these cases, the budget and associated work and schedule may be subject to change.

5.2.5 Objective measures of progress

The key to performance measurement is the objective assessment of work in progress. All work is completed, in progress or not yet started.

Completed work presents no performance measurement problem, since these work packages have been closed. Future work will not be measured until the work gets under way. The only work packages to be concerned about are those that are planned to be or are actually in progress at the end of the reporting period. The difficulty of assessment of those packages will lie largely in the level of detail and the earnings method that has been selected.

If the earning method is objective and is tied to schedule activities, then the job is straightforward and can be automated. If the earnings method is subjective or tied to events denoting a percentage completion, then a manual assessment will be necessary while a work package is in progress (also referred to as being 'open').

Judgements have to be made every reporting cycle from analysis by the project team on aspects of achievement, risk status and work to complete. Short work packages will make the assessment of achievement easier, but do not introduce arbitrary breaks in job planning and scheduling to shorten the work package duration as this goes against the objectiveness goal of EVM.

5.2.5.1 Measuring earned value

There are several approaches or methods of measuring earned value, known as earned value techniques (EVTs). The method used is dependent on the type of work being performed. Although a mixture of methods can be used on a single project, a work package or activity can be assigned only a single method. Once the work package has been opened, the method should not be changed.

Assignment of the EVT should be made at the work package level and consolidated through the WBS and OBS up to the total project level. Measurement of performance should be taken at the lowest practicable level to support the EVT.

The following sections highlight some of the commonly used methods. It should be remembered that hybrid methods can be developed, as long as they are objective, and representative of the way that the work is planned to be undertaken.

5.2.5.2 Milestones complete

Achievement of the work package is measured by the achievement of milestones.

Each milestone is assigned a proportion of the budget, and when the milestone is achieved, that proportion of the budget has been earned. This method of calculating earned value works best when there are a large number of frequent milestones. Earned value is only taken on milestone completion. If the number of milestones is low, then the measuring process becomes too coarse and is no longer useful to the project manager.

5.2.5.3 Percentage complete

Earned value is determined by the CAM's assessment of work in progress. This technique may be applied to activities with duration spanning three or more reporting periods and **where an objective basis exists for determining percentage complete for the work package.**

5.2.5.4 Equivalent units

This method is based on measuring the number of units or items that have been completed and comparing the result with the total number of units or items that have to be completed.

This approach is normally used in manufacturing, where the BCWP is measured as the number of units produced – for example, if large quantities of a particular item are being produced. This method is not particularly suited to development activity unless it has a repetitive element.

5.2.5.5 Formula method

The formula method is used where performance for low-value/non-critical material and other direct cost categories can be earned on the basis of actual cost, multiplied by the relationship of the budget at completion (BAC) to the EAC:

$$BCWP = ACWP \times BAC/EAC$$

This relies on a monthly update of the EAC to be accurate. It is useful in situations where progress can genuinely be directly related to spend – e.g. consumables, direct line feed. Table 5.1 provides examples of BCWP after applying the formula method based on a BAC value of 1000 units.

Table 5.1 BCWP calculations based on the formula method

Month	1	2	3	4	5
ACWP	200	400	700	1000	1400
EAC	1000	1000	1200	1300	1400
BCWP	200	400	583	769	1000

5.2.5.6 Level of effort

Level of effort (LoE) work packages are those within a project which are necessary for the project to be successful, but which do not have a specific end result or product and are not directly related to the generation of a specific result or product. Possible examples of such activities include some aspects of project management and contract administration. However, many of these activities, e.g. quality assurance and configuration management, should use the apportioned effort earned value technique (section 5.2.5.7).

Since LoE earned value is measured by the passage of time, it is important to ensure that the time-phased budget distribution is representative of the baseline schedule. Thus the achievement of the BCWP is always set equal to the BCWS, even if the work package has not started. This means schedule variances never occur, and hence LoE tasks do not allow meaningful earned value schedule analysis to be carried out.

However, LoE work packages can generate a cost variance (CV), and recorded ACWP can still be meaningfully compared to the BCWP.

LoE work packages should be separately defined from other work packages to avoid distorting any earned value analysis.

The LoE technique should be used only for those activities where no recovery action would be taken if the work were not undertaken.

5.2.5.7   Apportioned effort

Apportioned effort is effort that by itself is not readily divisible into short packages but is directly related to, and dependent upon measurable progress within another work package.

Apportioned effort is normally used for tasks such as inspection (during manufacturing). The link between an apportioned account and a base account is a schedule link: this means that the schedule in the apportioned account is derived by analogy to the work schedule of the base account, and the earnings in the apportioned account are derived by analogy to the work accomplished in the base account.

Earned value is determined by an apportioned factor (AF) calculated from the BAC for the apportioned and reference work package. The apportioned BCWS and apportioned BCWP is calculated by applying the apportionment factor as follows:

$$\text{apportioned BCWS} = \text{reference work package BCWS} \times \text{AF}$$
$$\text{apportioned BCWP} = \text{reference work package BCWP} \times \text{AF}$$

There is no similar apportionment of ACWP values for apportioned effort type work packages. Actual costs are directly recorded and reported against the work package, resulting in the generation of cost variances where they exist. Hence:

$$\text{ACWP} = \text{actual cost incurred from accounting system}$$

The control account manager of the apportioned account still controls the assignment of budget to the account, but the time-phasing of that budget and the percentage of earnings are driven by the base account.

The use of apportioned effort is demonstrated in Table 5.2.

Table 5.2 Apportioned work package calculations based on AF = 0.33

Reference work	BCWS	0	60	120	210	
package	BCWP	0	0	60	120	210
	ACWP	0	30	70	120	250
Apportioned work	BCWS	0	20	40	70	
package AF = 0.33	BCWP	0	0	20	40	70
	ACWP	0	10	40	50	65

5.2.5.8   Earned value types for material items:

Earned value measurement for material is measured like any other element of cost. It is thus intended to permit assessment of events that reflect progress in project performance, not measurement of administrative or financial events (e.g. booking of actual costs or invoice payment). Therefore, BCWS should normally be scheduled in accordance with a project event and BCWP should be earned when the event occurs. Administrative or financial events may be used as indicators for contract events when such indicators occur in the same reporting period as the contract events.

5.2.6   Baselining the project

When the plan is sufficiently developed and stable, it is frozen and agreed as the PMB. This PMB forms the basis for measuring all future progress and performance, and consequently allows the project to be managed.

The plan should include all elements of the project. The PMB consists of an approved set of baseline data, including all DB, schedules and EVTs for all work packages and planning packages, together with UB.

Periodic progress updates should be used to record progress, not to update and change the plan. All project team members should be actively using and reporting against a common plan.

Any additional plans, or significant changes to an established plan, should undergo a formal approval process before they become a baseline plan.

The key to having a proper management system is to ensure that the baseline plan represents the authorised execution for the project. This may be achieved by conducting an integrated baseline review (IBR) – see section 6.1.

5.2.7   Key activities in planning

1. Identify master milestones and deliverables.
2. Develop activities/milestones with logic dependencies, and durations.
3. Group activities to work packages and planning packages.
4. Apply resources (labour, material, subcontracts, other direct costs) to activities.
5. Distribute the appropriate budget across the work packages and planning packages contained within the control account.
6. Determine and assign the appropriate earned value type for the work packages.
7. Establish performance measurement baseline under configuration control.

5.3   DATA COLLECTION

What is the cost to the organisation of the project activities? The *data collection* processes are concerned with ensuring that complete and accurate cost information is collected in a timely manner to enable the transfer of actual cost information into the earned value management system.

5.3.1   Measuring costs and committed costs

The ACWP used in the earned value calculations include:

- labour costs (direct costs and indirect costs);
- direct expenses;
- material costs;
- subcontractor costs of work done.

Actual costs should be collected at a level that will identify the cost elements and factors contributing to cost variance. ACWP should be recorded in a manner consistent with the budget and should include all expenditure.

Ensure that BCWS, BCWP and ACWP are created in the same time frame.

Section 5.2.5.8 discussed earned value measurement for material. It may not be possible to ensure that earned value is claimed in the same period that actual costs are applied. In these cases, the company may choose to use estimated actual costs (or accruals) in the earned value management system, and the associated reports. A procedure should be in place to cover the process, and the subsequent replacement with 'real' costs.

As costs can be transferred or mis-booked during a period, it is recommended that cumulative costs be used in any calculations. Costs for the period should therefore be calculated as the difference between the cumulative costs last period and the current cumulative costs.

5.3.2.   KEY ACTIVITIES IN DATA COLLECTION

1. Ensure that procedures are in place to protect the integrity of bookings to work packages/control accounts and soon – i.e. the correct numbering system is set up (based upon the WBS) and correct booking/charge numbers are available to book to as required.
2. Use the estimated actuals process as required to ensure that there are no variances due to payment lag.
3. Verify actual costs to ensure only valid costs are booked to valid booking/charge numbers.

5.4   ANALYSIS, REVIEW AND ACTION

How well are we performing against the baseline plan, and what actions are required? This section is concerned with the evaluation of the measured performance as compared to the baseline plan. Appropriate management and customer reports (e.g. cost performance reports) will be generated, together with the identification and implementation of management actions.

5.4.1 Schedule status

It is essential to update the status of schedules in a timely manner to gain an objective understanding of the achievement of milestones and deliverables, and to monitor how task dependencies are affected by any task movement.
  When updating the schedule status, the following should be considered:

- activity actual start/finish dates;
- estimate of time remaining to complete the task;
- estimated start and finish dates for future activities.

Schedule status may then be determined by comparing how much time the activity is ahead of or behind the baseline schedule.
  The following aspects of schedule assessment may be performed at both detail and project level:

- review of the critical path activities;
- review of schedule against key milestone forecasts;
- review of future resource requirements.

5.4.2 Calculating and reporting earned value

5.4.2.1 How to calculate variances/indices

All variances are measured in terms of cost and apply equally to all methods of measurement. There are five types of variances/indices commonly used.

SV   **Schedule variance** – the cost comparison of what has been earned to what was budgeted. It measures the difference in value between the work planned and the work actually accomplished:

$$SV = BCWP - BCWS$$
$$SV\% = (SV/BCWS) \times 100$$

CV   **Cost variance** – the cost comparison of what has been earned to what has been spent:

$$CV = BCWP - ACWP$$
$$CV\% = (CV/BCWP) \times 100$$

VAC   **Variance at completion** – the cost comparison of the budget at completion with the current estimate at completion:

$$VAC = BAC - EAC$$
$$VAC\% = (VAC/BAC) \times 100$$

SPI   **Schedule performance index** – an indication of how far behind or ahead of the planned work the project is (in terms of the value of the work accomplished); it tends towards 1.0 as the project progresses. It is of less value as the project nears completion:

$$SPI = BCWP/BCWS$$

CPI   **Cost performance index** – the index of earned value to actual costs. Below 1.0 is unfavourable; above 1.0 is favourable:

$$CPI = BCWP/ACWP$$

In addition to these variances being shown on a cumulative spend graph, the indices can also be plotted cumulatively through the life of a project to show improving (or worsening) performance.

5.4.2.2   Reporting graphs

Figure 5.6 demonstrates the performance of a project using the earned value data elements. It provides a quick view of project status and prevailing trends. It may be used as a basis for forecasting the project end conditions. It can also include, if required, the EAC and the forecast completion date for the previous reporting periods.

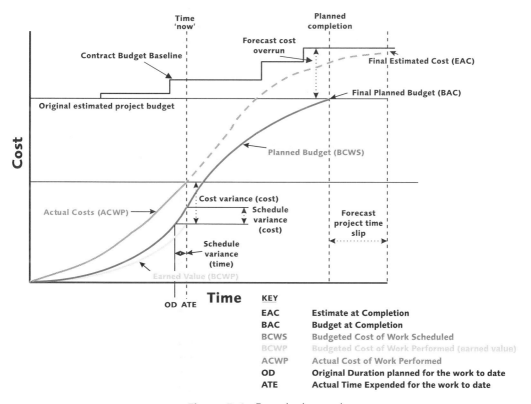

Figure 5.6 – Earned value graph

27

5.4.2.3 Variance thresholds

It is strongly recommended that variance thresholds be established. This will ensure that not all variances need be printed or explained in detail at each reporting cycle. These thresholds are set to minimise the detail included in reports when there are only minor variances.

If any of the values being monitored fall within predefined limits then full details are not required on the variances. However, when any of the variances fall outside the thresholds then a full variance analysis, together with methods of recovery, should be reported.

Thresholds can be set as a value, as a percentage or both. The values set for each project will be decided by the size, complexity, risk and so on of each project. It is normal for separate thresholds to be set for last reporting period and cumulative performance. Consideration should also be given to the convergence of thresholds over the life of the project.

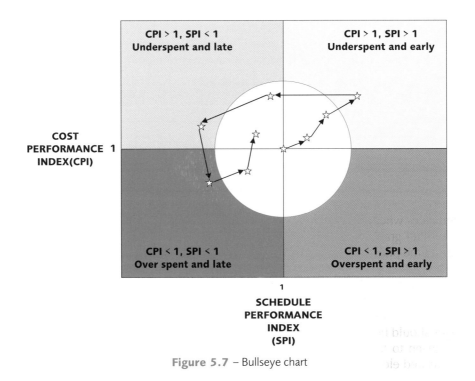

Figure 5.7 – Bullseye chart

5.4.2.4 Performance trend charts

The bullseye chart (Figure 5.7) shows the change in schedule performance index and cost performance index at each reporting period. The graph gives a summary view as to whether performance is improving or deteriorating and

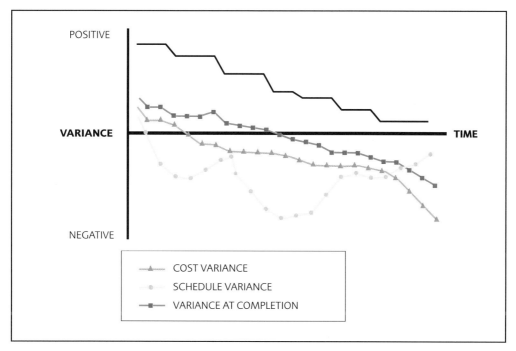

POSITIVE

VARIANCE ——————————————————————— TIME

NEGATIVE

- —▲— COST VARIANCE
- ⊙ SCHEDULE VARIANCE
- —■— VARIANCE AT COMPLETION

Figure 5.8 – Variance trend graphs

whether the variances are outside the agreed thresholds. The central circle shows the maximum variance thresholds. The CPI and SPI are plotted on the graph at each reporting cycle in the project.

An alternative approach to the bullseye chart is to show the change in schedule variance and cost variance on a time phase. Such a graph (figure 5.8) indicates whether performance is improving.

Another graph that can be used is the CPI/SPI curve that shows CPI and SPI on a time phase.

The assessment of performance through cost and schedule variance should take into account any potential 'washout' of any one budget type over another – e.g. where material cost is significantly higher than the cost of the labour required to process/use the material. In these instances, separate work packages should be created for material and labour. Similarly, consideration should be given to the separation of level of effort and indirect cost elements from measured elements.

5.4.3 Estimates at completion

An estimate at completion is the estimate of final cost based on realistic plans and assumptions by management and using the most current and accurate information available.

The EAC is the sum of the actual costs (ACWP) up to the present, plus the best estimates of the costs still to be incurred, (estimate to completion, ETC).

EACs are calculated and analysed at any level of the WBS or OBS. Thus:

$$EAC = ACWP_{Cumulative} + ETC$$

There are several methods for generating EACs, some of which are described in Appendix D. These should be used in conjunction with the comprehensive bottom-up EACs developed at control account level.

The following should be considered when defining a detailed EAC:

- past performance;
- required efficiency to recover;
- costs (incurred and committed) to date;
- the use of contract charging rates (incorporating overhead cost pools) to obtain the cost of labour based estimates;
- technical assessment of tasks remaining;
- cost and schedule variances incurred to date;
- expected future efficiency;
- percentage of task already completed and remaining risks (risk review and probability of cost impact);
- ongoing or outstanding management actions;
- forecast schedule completion of the task;
- anticipated changes to the scope of work;
- future economic conditions, forecast rate changes and escalation indices;
- previous EAC trend.

5.4.3.1 Simple tests of reasonableness

As well as the above formulae, there are several tests of reasonableness that can be applied to project data.

Current performance indicators (SPI, CPI) will provide a 'performance to date' view of the project. *To complete performance index* (TCPI) allows a projection of the anticipated performance to achieve either the BAC or the EAC (dependent on which formula is employed) – i.e., what level of performance needs to be achieved to meet the BAC or EAC.

A figure greater than 1.0 indicates that future efficiency will need to be greater than planned, conversely less than 1.0 indicates future efficiency may be less than planned to achieve BAC or EAC (dependent on which formula is employed).

TCPI should also be compared with the CPI. This can provide additional performance information. If the TCPI is greater than the current CPI, future efficiency must improve if the project is to achieve the BAC/EAC.

Table 5.3 demonstrates the use of TCPI.

Table 5.3 Example of projecting anticipated performance using TCPI (BAC) and TCPI (EAC)

	Period				
	1	2	3	4	5
BCWS	10	20	50	80	120
BCWP	10	10	20	60	100
ACWP	12	15	30	80	110
BAC	120	120	120	120	120
EAC	120	130	160	150	130
CPI	0.83	0.67	0.67	0.75	0.91
TCPI (BAC)	1.02	1.05	1.11	1.50	2.00
TCPI (EAC)	1.02	0.96	0.77	0.86	1.00

In this example, for period 3 a TCPI (BAC) of 1.11 is required to complete the remainder of the work within the budget at completion. When this is compared with the current CPI of 0.67, it is clear that significant performance improvements are required if this is to be achieved. However, a CPI of 0.77 is required to complete the remainder of the work, within the estimate at completion. By comparison with the prevailing CPI (0.67) this may be achievable, with some consistent performance improvement. It may be seen by looking at period 2 data that the required performance improvement – current CPI of 0.67 to TCPI (EAC) 0.96 – is unachievable; this should prompt a re-evaluation of the viability of the EAC.

To corroborate the accuracy of forecasted costs there are two approaches:

$$EAC = BAC/CPI$$
$$ETC = (BAC - BCWP)/CPI$$

To check forecast completion dates (in weeks from project start):

$$forecast\ completion = original\ completion/SPI$$

For a full description of the earned value formulae, see Appendix D.

5.4.4   Key activities in analysis, review and action

1. Update control accounts with achievement, in line with the calendar.
2. Update schedule status and schedule forecasts, in line with the calendar.
3. Determine estimate to completion as required.
4. Integrate whole project, to determine impact on critical path (if used).
5. Analyse variances to baseline, and focus on problem areas.
6. Take corrective action as required.

5.5 CHANGE MANAGEMENT

The change management process ensures change is assessed and incorporated into the project baseline in a timely and controlled manner. This section considers the controlled processes whereby the project formally maintains the integrity of the contract budget baseline and the performance measurement baseline. It is important that all changes to past, present and future information are embodied in the PMB in an orderly and documented manner, so that it remains an accurate representation of all authorised work.

The approved project baseline is the time-phased budget against which project progress and performance are measured and reported. This baseline is used as the budgeted cost of work scheduled.

A baseline plan defines not only the financial baseline and structures for a project but also the timescales, resources and boundary of the plan.

Changes to the current baseline must be strictly controlled in order to maintain a valid basis for project performance assessment. The current baseline must be traceable back to the original baseline, and be reconcilable to the current authorised scope, schedule and cost objectives.

Changes to the current baseline should not be made because of an overspend or a delay. Conditions that may warrant a change to the baseline include for example:

- an authorised change to the scope, cost or schedule of the project;
- changes to standard rates (e.g. labour, material or overhead);
- work and budget transfer between control accounts.

Baselines are updated by adding extra budget for additional work scope and/or transferring management reserve into the budget baseline. MR budget can be transferred only with management approval. All transfers should be documented and authorised.

The additional budgets can be incorporated into the project as follows:

- new work packages can be generated solely for the budget transferred;
- existing work packages can be closed and new work packages opened to include the outstanding work plus the additional budget.

Additional budget should not be assigned to a closed work package. If the current baseline is being amended, history should not be changed; the focus should be on establishing a workable plan for the accomplishment of the remaining efforts.

5.5.1 Key activities in change management

1. Identify and raise necessary changes to the control account.
2. Integrate, where applicable, change to associated risks.

3. Ensure that all changes to the PMB are reflected within the associated forecast plans.
4. Ensure that changes are embodied within all elements of management system (toolset, documentation, reports etc.).
5. Seek appropriate approval for change.

5.6 RISK MANAGEMENT

The integration of EVM and risk management should provide more realistic earned value assessments and give a better estimate of the project completion cost and timescale.

Project Risk Analysis and Management is a process which enables the analysis and management of the risks associated with a project. Properly undertaken it will increase the likelihood of successful completion of a project to cost, time and performance objectives. It should be regarded as an integral part of project or business management and not just as a set of tools or techniques. (Association for Project Management, 2000)

The benefits of systematic risk identification and risk management (RM) include:

- more realistic business and project planning;
- actions being implemented in time to be effective;
- greater certainty of achieving business goals and project objectives;
- appreciation of, and readiness to exploit, all beneficial opportunities;
- improved loss control;
- improved control of project and business costs;
- increased flexibility as a result of understanding all options and their associated risks;
- greater control over innovation and business development;
- fewer costly surprises through effective and transparent contingency planning.

The above list has been reproduced from BS6079-3:2000 (British Standards, Institution, 2000b). As may be seen, the benefits are almost identical to those attributed to earned value management in section 1.

Earned value management and risk management are complementary processes. Both are key aspects of the overall project management discipline. Risk management is largely related to what may happen in the future; earned value management is concerned with using what has already happened to predict and control the future. There may be great synergies to be realised by integrating the two processes.

The following list suggests areas where risk management may be usefully integrated with earned value management:

- estimating the project activities (cost and schedule):
  – project activities;
  – risk mitigation activities;
  – contingency activities;
- establishing management reserve budget;
- creating and controlling the budget and schedule for the RM process – i.e. those elements of the overall project management activities that cover risk management (not to be confused with the MR budget);
- scheduling:
  – incorporating RM activities in the baseline schedule;
  – establishing dependencies;
  – determining risk inherent within schedule by using statistical risk network analysis;
  – risk modelling to optimise project schedules;
- including RM activities in project performance analysis:
  – including resource, cost and schedule for risk management activities in overall project earned value;
  – using earned value to determine the performance of the risk management activities, e.g. identifying if the mitigation plan is likely to be achieved on time and to budget;
- development of forecasts:
  – estimate at completion (cost);
  – schedule forecast (time);
  – modelling with the risk network;
- change management: incorporation of MR budget for contingency activities.

If the EVM system has been established in accordance with this guide, then the key integrating structures will have been defined, namely the work breakdown structure and the project schedule/network. These structures are ideal for storing and defining information about the project and would therefore provide logical and convenient structures for risk reporting. Each element in the structure contains the data that is commonly used to inform quantitative risk analysis and would also provide a convenient place for noting qualitative risks at the point where they are likely to occur. Further, if the structure defines the whole project then a complete risk checklist can be stored and compiled with no danger of oversight.

In 2008 APM published further guidance, *Interfacing Risk and Earned Value Management*.

This takes the approach that the key to EVM and RM interfacing lies in the recognition that added value can be found in both disciplines through commonality of purpose in setting, measuring and achieving project targets. A baseline that takes no account of risk is extremely unlikely to be achieved; similarly, risk response actions that are not resourced and effectively monitored are unlikely to produce the desired results.

The guide has set out to establish the principles and potential practices for a closer relationship between the EVM and RM disciplines. These principles can be used to develop and inform the advancement of organisations, RM and EVM capability.

5.6.1 Key activities in risk management

1. Risk identification
2. Risk assessment
3. Produce response strategy

6
System review

Once an EVMS has been established it is considered good practice to review the system in order to ensure that it is being operated effectively, and is compliant with recognised standards (the EVM criteria). The reviews may be demanded and conducted by a customer; alternatively, many companies operate an internal process against the same standards.

The earned value management reviews provide confirmation of an early capture of scope, quantifying it in terms of cost and schedule with the structure to manage it in a controlled manner from there on. A thorough review will identify areas of weak planning, enabling improvements early on. It is important that reviews are conducted professionally.

Earned value reviews provide several benefits:

1. They confirm that an *integrated project management system* exists.
2. They will provide a *fixed cut-off point* to conclude the planning phase.
3. They are pre-planned checkpoints. They validate reliable performance data, thus avoiding wasted subsequent work based on unsound information.
4. They reduce *risk*.
5. They should ensure that *historic experience* from previous projects is captured.
6. They can be an effective tool to put the focus on performance measurement.

The three main categories of EVM system reviews are discussed below.

6.1   INTEGRATED BASELINE REVIEW (IBR)

In order to review the quality of the developed baseline plan, an **integrated baseline review** should be held as soon as possible after the project has gone through at least one reporting cycle following the establishment of the initial baseline. This ensures that performance data is available during the review.

An IBR is a formal process conducted to assess the content and integrity of the PMB. It should ensure the timely establishment of the integrated technical, cost and schedule baseline. It determines the credibility, sufficiency and adequacy of the planning, and ensures that activities are integrated with each other. The ultimate purpose of the IBR is to achieve and maintain a project, as well as and customer understanding of the risks inherent in the PMB and the management control processes that will operate during its execution.

The conduct of the review process should not be restricted to project personnel but should cover all personnel, both project and customer, that are critical to the successful achievement of the project's objectives.

Further detail on the purpose and conduct of an IBR is contained in Reference 5.

6.2   DEMONSTRATION REVIEW

In order to examine the new project management system, a ***demonstration review*** may be held. This is different from an IBR because it reviews the total system, looking particularly at the system operations. The EVMS is checked fully for compliance against all the earned value criteria.

In addition to the EVMS review, data traces and interviews are undertaken. Covering areas that play a role in operating the system are included, such as finance and project controls, as well as the managers.

This time, the EVMS is assessed against all the EV guidelines. The demonstration review report is written during the review, based on the five guideline groups of:

- organisation;
- planning, scheduling and budgeting;
- accounting;
- analysis and management reports;
- revisions and data maintenance.

It highlights where the system is working well and addresses the discrepancy reports on system deficiencies.

6.3   SURVEILLANCE

In order to confirm that standards are being maintained, periodic surveillance should be conducted throughout the remainder of the project.

Like any dynamic control system, there is always a possibility that the project may run out of control: with an EVMS, it can sometimes be easy for the project to fall into complacency and let the management system run without doing any further data checks highlighting any data integrity problems. At this stage of the project there are likely to have been substantial changes made to the project's system. These will include changes aimed at improving the system which will need to be reviewed to ensure they are still in accordance with the EV guidelines of the criteria set out in Appendix A.

There is also the possibility that both management and CAMs have undergone considerable change. New managers need to be interviewed to ensure that they are fully conversant with the management of earned value.

Surveillance must ensure that the project's EVMS:

- provides timely and reliable cost, schedule and technical performance information summarised directly from the project's internal management system;
- complies with the EVM guidelines;
- provides timely indications of actual or potential problems;
- maintains baseline integrity;
- provides information that depicts actual conditions and trends;
- provides comprehensive variance analysis at the appropriate levels, including proposed corrective action with regard to cost, schedule and technical performance, and other problem areas.

Bibliography

Useful publications include the following.

- American National Standards Institute/Electronic Industries Alliance (1998) *Industry Guidelines for Earned Value Management Systems,* ANSI/EIA–748-1998
- Association for Project Management (2000) *Project Risk Analysis and Management Guide*
- Association for Project Management (2006) *APM Body of Knowledge,* 5th edn
- Association for Project Management (2008) *Interfacing Risk and Earned Value Management*
- British Standards Institution (2000a) *Project Management: Guide to Project Management,* BS6079-1: 2000
- British Standards Institution (2000b) *Project Management: Guide to the Management of Business Related Project Risk,* BS6079-3: 2000
- US Department of Defense (1998) *Department of Defense Handbook: Work Breakdown Structure,* MIL-HDBK-881
- Defence Earned Value Management Implementation Group IBR Sub-committee (2005) A Guide to Conducting Integrated Baseline Reviews, URL: http://www.aof.mod.uk/aofcontent/tactical/ppm/downloads/evm/uk IBR Review Guide Issue 2 January 2005.doc

Appendix A
Earned value
management guidelines

This section provides the basic criteria for projects to use in establishing and operating an integrated earned value management system. The criteria concept does not describe a system but a set of criteria that are intended to state the qualities and operational considerations of a project management system using earned value management without mandating system-level characteristics.

It is expected that compliance with the requirements detailed herein will allow key stakeholders, notably customers and shareholders, to gain confidence that projects are being managed and resources deployed in an effective manner.

The criteria require projects' management control systems to provide data which:

- provides timely and reliable information about work progress;
- properly relates cost, schedule and technical achievement;
- supplies managers with information at a practical level of summarisation.

The criteria have been reproduced with minor amendments from the industry standard (American National Standards Institute, 1998) and are organised in five major categories.

A.1 ORGANISATION

1. Define the authorised work elements for the project. A work breakdown structure (WBS), tailored for effective internal management control, is commonly used in this process.
   Paraphrase of criterion: Define authorised work and resources via contract work breakdown structure (CWBS).
2. Identify the project organisational structure, including the major subcontractors responsible for achieving the authorised work, and define the organisational elements in which work will be planned and controlled.
   Paraphrase of criterion: Establish organisational responsibility for work achievement via OBS.
3. Provide for the integration of the project's planning, scheduling, budgeting, work authorisation and cost accumulation processes with each other and, as

appropriate, the work breakdown structure and the organisational structure.

Paraphrase of Criterion: Ensure management subsystems support each other, the CWBS and the OBS.

4. Identify the organisation responsible for controlling overhead (indirect costs).

   Paraphrase of criterion: Identify who is responsible for overhead cost control.

5. Provide for integration of the project work breakdown structure and the project organisational structure in a manner that permits cost and schedule performance measurement by elements of either or both structures as needed.

   Paraphrase of Criterion: Integrate CWBS with OBS.

A.2 PLANNING, SCHEDULING AND BUDGETING

6. Schedule the authorised work in a manner that describes the sequence of work and identifies significant task interdependencies required to meet the requirements of the project.

   Paraphrase of criterion: Schedule all authorised work logically.

7. Identify physical products, milestones, technical performance goals or other indicators that will be used to measure progress.

   Paraphrase of criterion: Identify interim goals (milestones) by which to measure work achievement.

8. Establish and maintain a time-phased budget baseline, at the control account level, against which project performance can be measured. Budget for far-term efforts may be held in higher-level accounts until an appropriate time for allocation at the control account level. Initial budgets established for performance measurement will be based on either internal management goals or the external customer negotiated target cost including estimates for authorised but undefinitised work. If an over-target baseline (OTB) is used for performance measurement reporting purposes, prior notification must be provided to the appropriate senior manager and customer (if required).

   Paraphrase of criterion: Establish/maintain at the control account level a performance measurement baseline.

9. Establish budgets for authorised work, with identification of significant cost elements (labour, material etc.) as needed for internal management and for control of subcontractors.

   Paraphrase of criterion: Establish budgets by element of cost.

10. To the extent it is practical to identify the authorised work in discrete work packages, establish budgets for this work in terms of money, hours, or other measurable units. Where the entire control account is not subdivided into

work packages, identify the far-term effort in larger planning packages for budget and scheduling purposes.

Paraphrase of criterion: Establish budgets at the work/planning package level.

11. Provide that the sum of all work package budgets plus planning package budgets within a control account equals the control account budget.

    Paraphrase of criterion: Sum of all WP + PP budget = Budget$_{CA}$.

12. Identify and control level of effort activity by time-phased budgets established for this purpose. Only that effort which is unmeasurable or for which measurement is impractical may be classified as level of effort.

    Paraphrase of criterion: Separately identify and control the use of LoE.

13. Establish overhead budgets for each significant organisational component of the company for expenses which will become indirect costs. Reflect in the project budgets, at the appropriate level, the amounts in overhead pools that are planned to be allocated to the project as indirect costs.

    Paraphrase of criterion: Establish budgets for overhead costs.

14. Identify management reserves and undistributed budget.

    Paraphrase of criterion: Identify MR and UB separately.

15. Provide that the project target cost goal is reconciled with the sum of all internal project budgets and management reserves.

    Paraphrase of criterion: CBB = BAC + MR.

A.3   ACCOUNTING CONSIDERATIONS

16. Record direct costs in a manner consistent with the budgets in a formal system controlled by the general books of account.

    Paraphrase of criterion: Formally record all direct costs and establish budgets in a consistent and thus comparable manner.

17. Summarise direct costs from control accounts into the work breakdown structure without allocation of a single control account to two or more work breakdown structure elements.

    Paraphrase of criterion: Prohibit multiple accounting as direct costs are summarised through the WBS.

18. Summarise direct costs from the control accounts into the organisational structure without allocation of a single control account to two or more organisational elements.

    Paraphrase of criterion: Prohibit multiple accounting as direct costs are summarised through the OBS.

19. Record all indirect costs that will be allocated to the contract.

    Paraphrase of criterion: Record all allocable indirect costs.

20. Identify unit costs, equivalent unit costs or lot costs when needed.

    Paraphrase of criterion: Identify applicable unit costs.

21. For EVMS, the material accounting system will provide for:

(1) accurate cost accumulation and assignment of costs to control accounts in a manner consistent with the budgets using recognised, acceptable, costing techniques;

(2) cost performance measurement at the point in time most suitable for the category of material involved, but no earlier than the time of progress payments or actual receipt of material;

(3) full accountability of all material purchased for the project including the residual inventory.

Paraphrase of criterion: Establish an acceptable material accounting system.

A.4   ANALYSIS AND MANAGEMENT REPORTS

22. At least on a monthly basis, generate the following information at the control account and other levels as necessary for management control using actual cost data from, or reconcilable with, the accounting system:

   (1) comparison of the amount of planned budget and the amount of budget earned for work achieved–this comparison provides the schedule variance;

   (2) comparison of the amount of the budget earned and the actual (applied/estimated where appropriate) direct costs for the same work – this comparison provides the cost variance.

   Paraphrase of criterion: Identify performance measurement data elements at the CA level on a monthly basis.

23. Identify, at least monthly, the significant differences between both planned and actual schedule performance and planned and actual cost performance, and provide the reasons for the variances in the detail needed by project management.

   Paraphrase of criterion: Identify schedule and cost deviations on at least a monthly basis.

24. Identify budgeted and applied (or actual) indirect costs at the level and frequency needed by management for effective control, along with the reasons for any significant variances.

   Paraphrase of criterion: Identify overhead performance measurement data as needed.

25. Summarise the data elements and associated variances through the project organisation and/or work breakdown structure to support management needs and any customer reporting specified in the contract.

   Paraphrase of criterion: Sum performance measurement data elements through the CWBS and OBS.

26. Implement managerial actions taken as the result of earned value information.

   Paraphrase of criterion: Identify management response to variances.

27. Develop revised estimates of cost at completion based on performance to date, commitment values for material and estimates of future conditions. Compare this information with the performance measurement baseline to identify variances at completion important to company management and any applicable customer reporting requirements.
Paraphrase of criterion: Develop EACs and compare with staffing plans and the CBB.

A.5   REVISIONS AND DATA MAINTENANCE

28. Incorporate authorised changes in a timely manner, recording the effects of such changes in budgets and schedules. In the directed effort prior to negotiation of a change, base such revisions on the amount estimated and budgeted to the project organisations.
Paraphrase of criterion: Incorporate all authorised changes in a timely manner.

29. Reconcile current budgets to prior budgets in terms of changes to the authorised work and internal replanning in the detail needed by management for effective control.
Paraphrase of criterion: Reconcile original budgets with current budgets.

30. Control retroactive changes to records pertaining to work performed that would change previously reported amounts for actual costs, earned value or budgets. Adjustments should be made only for correction of errors, routine accounting adjustments, effects of customer or management directed changes, or to improve the baseline integrity and accuracy of performance measurement data.
Paraphrase of criterion: Control retroactive changes to records.

31. Prevent revisions to the project budget except for authorised changes.
Paraphrase of criterion: Only the senior manager or the customer may revise the CBB.

32. Document changes to the performance measurement baseline.
Paraphrase of criterion: Document PMB changes.

Appendix B
Terminology
and glossary

Activity. An element of work performed during the course of a project. An activity normally has an expected duration, an expected cost and expected resource requirements. Activities are often subdivided into tasks.

Actual cost. The costs actually incurred and recorded in accomplishing work performed.

Actual cost of work performed (ACWP). The costs actually incurred and recorded in achieving the work performed.

Allocated budget. *See* **total allocated budget.**

Applied direct costs. The actual direct costs recognised in the time period associated with the consumption of labour, material and other direct resources, without regard to the date of commitment or the date of payment. These amounts are to be charged to work-in-process when any of the following takes place:

- labour, material or other direct resources are actually consumed;

- material resources are withdrawn from inventory for use;

- material resources are received that are uniquely identified to the contract; or

- major components or assemblies that are specifically and uniquely identified to a single serially numbered end item are received on a line flow basis.

Apportioned effort. Effort that by itself is not readily measured or divisible into discrete work packages but which is related in direct proportion to the planning and performance on other measured effort.

Authorised unpriced work (AUW). Includes work that has been authorised, but for which the cost has not been finalised by virtue of a formal contract amendment.

Authorised work. All work performed, pursuant to the contract, within the contract price.

Baseline. *See* **performance measurement baseline.**

Budget. The resources (in money and/or hours) assigned for the accomplishment of a specific task or group of tasks.

Budget at completion (BAC). The total authorised budget for achieving the project scope of work. It is equal to the sum of all allocated budgets plus any undistributed budget (management reserve is not included).

Budgeted cost of work performed (BCWP). The sum of the budgets for completed work packages and completed portions of open work packages, plus the applicable portion of the budgets for level of effort and apportioned effort.

Budgeted cost of work scheduled (BCWS). The sum of the budgets for all work packages, planning packages etc. scheduled to be achieved (including in-process work packages), plus the amount of level of effort and apportioned effort scheduled to be achieved. This may be expressed as the BCSW within a given time period, such as period BCWS or cumulative BCWS.

Budgets for work packages. *See* **work-package budgets.**

Commitment. That portion of purchased items or services which has been ordered, but for which no actuals have been incurred.

Contract budget baseline (CBB). The contract target cost plus the estimated cost of authorised unpriced work.

Contract price. The price payable by the customer under the contract for the proper delivery of the supplies and services specified in the scope of work of the contract.

Contract target cost. The total of the sum of all control accounts plus undistributed budget plus management reserve.

Contract work breakdown structure (CWBS). The complete WBS for a contract, developed and used by a contractor according to the contract work statement. The CWBS includes the levels specified in the contract.

Control account (CA). A management control point at which actual costs can be accumulated and compared with earned value and budgets (resource plans) for management control purposes. A control account is a natural management point for cost/schedule planning and control since it represents the work assigned to one responsible organisational element for one contract work breakdown structure (CWBS) element.

Control account manager (CAM). The performing manager who is responsible for planning, performing and monitoring the elements of work defined within that control account.

Cost performance report. A contractually required report, prepared by the contractor, containing information derived from the internal system. Provides status of progress on the contract.

Cost variance (CV). A metric for the cost performance of a project. It is the algebraic difference between earned value and actual cost (CV = BCWP − ACWP).

A positive value indicates a favourable position and a negative value indicates an unfavourable position.

Critical path analysis. A network analysis technique used to predict project duration by analysing which sequence of activities (which path) has the least amount of scheduling flexibility (the least amount of float). Early dates are calculated by means of a forward pass using a specified start date. Late dates are calculated by means of a backward pass starting from a specified completion date (usually the forward pass's calculated project early finish date).

Direct costs. The costs of resources expended in the achievement of work, which are directly charged to the project, without inclusion of indirect costs.

Distributed budget (DB). All budgets that have been assigned to the control accounts. Distributed budget excludes management reserve and undistributed budget.

Earned value (EV). The value of completed work expressed in terms of the budget assigned to that work.

Earned value management (EVM). A best practice project control process that is based on a structured approach to planning, cost collection and performance measurement. It facilitates the integration of project scope, schedule, cost, risk and resource objectives, and the establishment of a baseline plan for performance measurement.

Earned value management system (EVMS). An integrated management system which uses earned value to measure progress objectively.

Earned value technique (EVT). A technique used to objectively assess progress.

Estimate at completion (EAC). Actual direct costs, plus indirect costs allocable to the contract, plus the estimate of costs (direct and indirect) for remaining authorised work.

Estimated actuals process. When material actual costs are not applied in the same period as earned value is claimed, an estimate of the material cost is placed in the earned value system until it is replaced in a subsequent period by 'real' costs.

Estimate to completion (ETC). The forecast of labour hours and costs required to complete the remaining authorised work. It is based on a bottom-up analysis of remaining work, and past and future performance, along with the availability of resources, is taken into consideration.

Final estimated cost. *See* **estimate at completion.**

Funding. The actual money available for expenditure in the achievement of contract work. The planning of work and the time-phasing of budgets and ETCs should be consistent with the known available funding for that period.

Indirect costs. The costs for common or joint objectives which cannot be identified specifically with a particular project or activity. Also referred to as overhead cost or burden.

Initial budget. *See* **original budget.**

Integrated baseline review (IBR). A formal process conducted to assess the content and integrity of the PMB. The purpose of the IBR is to achieve and maintain a project and customer understanding of the risks inherent in the PMB and the management control processes that will operate during its execution.

Level of effort (LoE). Effort of a general or supportive nature which does not produce definite end products. Earned value (BCWP) for LoE always equals the planned budget to date (BCWS) whether or not any work is performed.

Management reserve (MR). An amount of the total allocated budget withheld for management control purposes rather than designated for the achievement of a specific task or set of tasks. It is not a part of the performance measurement baseline.

Materiel. All non-labour classes of resource.

Milestone. An activity of zero duration, principally used to enhance the clarity of the project structure.

Organisation breakdown structure (OBS). A functionally oriented code established to identify the performance responsibility for work on a specific contract.

Original budget. The budget established at, or near, the time the contract was signed, based on the negotiated contract cost.

Original duration. The duration established at, or near, the time the contract was signed, based on the negotiated contract cost.

Other direct costs (ODC). A group of costs which can be identified to specific tasks, other than labour, material and subcontract. Included in ODC are such costs as travel, accommodation, insurance, computer time and services.

Over-target baseline (OTB). An agreed Contract Budget Baseline (CBB) which exceeds the contract target cost (CTC) against which a baseline is set to measure performance. When remaining budgets are deemed insufficient to complete the remaining work, the budgets may be increased by seeking approval in advance from the customer to report to a new total budget which exceeds the original contract budget base, or an over-target baseline. Now the total allocated budget equals the previous CBB plus the previously budgeted margin plus any contractor contribution.

Overhead. Indirect labour, material, supplies, services costs and other charges which cannot be consistently identified with individual projects. *See* Indirect Costs.

Performance measurement baseline (PMB). The time-phased budget plan against which contract performance is measured. It is formed by the budgets assigned to scheduled control accounts and the applicable indirect budgets. For future effort, not planned to the control account level, the performance measurement baseline also includes budgets assigned to higher-level CWBS elements and undistributed budgets. It equals the total allocated budget less management reserve.

Planning package (PP). A logical aggregation of work within a control account, normally the far-term effort, that can be identified and budgeted in early baseline planning, but is not yet defined into work packages.

Responsible organisation. A defined unit within the contractor's organisational structure which is assigned responsibility for achieving specific tasks.

Responsibility assignment matrix (RAM). A depiction of the relationship between the contract work breakdown structure elements and the organisations assigned responsibility for ensuring their accomplishment.

Risk management. A structured process that allows individual risk events and overall project risk to be understood and managed proactively, optimizing project success by minimizing threats and minimizing opportunities.

Rolling wave. The action of converting a planning package into a work package.

Schedule. The timing and sequence of tasks within a project, as well as the project duration. The schedule consists mainly of tasks, dependencies among tasks, durations, constraints, resources and time-oriented project information.

Schedule variance (SV). A metric for the schedule performance of a project. It is the difference between earned value and the budget (schedule variance = earned value − budget). A positive value is a favourable condition while a negative value is unfavourable.

Significant variances (SV). Those differences between planned and actual performance which require further review, analysis or action. Appropriate thresholds should be established as to the magnitude of variances that will automatically require variance analysis.

Statement of work (SOW). A narrative description of products or services to be delivered by the project.

Supplies. The goods and services, including intellectual property, required to be supplied under the contract.

Total allocated budget. The sum of all budgets allocated to the contract. Total allocated budget consists of the performance measurement baseline plus all management reserve. The total allocated budget reconciles directly to the contract budget base.

Undistributed budget (UB). Budget applicable to contract effort that has not yet been allocated into the performance measurement baseline or placed in reserve.

Variance at completion (VAC). The difference between the total budget assigned to a contract, WBS element, organisational entity or control account, and the estimate at completion. It represents the amount of expected overrun or underrun.

Variances. *See* **significant variances**.

Work breakdown structure (WBS). A product-oriented family-tree division of hardware, software, services and other work tasks which organises, defines and graphically displays the product to be produced, as well as the work to be done to achieve the specified product.

WBS dictionary. A description of all individual elements within each level of the WBS which is sufficient to define their scope, including tasks, dependencies and deliverables.

Work package (WPs). A group of related activities that are defined at the same level within a work breakdown structure.

Work-package budgets. Resources which are formally assigned by the contractor to achieve a work package, expressed in money, hours, standards or other measurable units.

Appendix C
Abbreviations
and acronyms

ACWP	Actual cost of work performed
AE	Apportioned effort
AF	Apportioned factor
ATE	Actual time expended
BAC	Budget at completion
BCWP	Budgeted cost of work performed
BCWR	Budgeted cost of work remaining
BCWS	Budgeted cost for work scheduled
CA	Control account, also known as cost account
CAM	Control account manager
CBB	Contract budget baseline
CPI	Cost performance index
CPM	Critical path method
CPR	Cost performance report
CTC	Contract target cost
CV	Cost variance
CV%	Cost variance percentage
CWBS	Contract work breakdown structure
DB	Distributed budget
EAC	Estimate at completion
ETC	Estimate to completion
EV	Earned value
EVA	Earned value analysis
EVM	Earned value management
EVMS	Earned value management system
EVT	Earned value technique
IBR	Integrated baseline review
LoE	Level of effort
LRE	Latest revised estimate (same as EAC)
MR	Management reserve
OBS	Organisation breakdown structure
OD	Original duration
ODC	Other direct costs
OTB	Over-target baseline
P_f	Performance factor
PMB	Performance measurement baseline

PMS	Project master schedule
PP	Planning package
PV	Planned value
RAM	Responsibility assignment matrix
RM	Risk management
SoR	Statement of requirement
SOW	Statement of work
SPI	Schedule performance index
SV	Schedule variance
SV%	Schedule variance percentage
TAB	Total allocated budget
TCPI	To complete performance index
UB	Undistributed budget
VAC	Variance at completion
VAC%	Variance at completion percentage
VAR	Variance analysis report
WBS	Work breakdown structure
WP	Work package

Appendix D
Earned value equations

D.1 BASIC FORMULAE

1. Cost variance

   CV = BCWP – ACWP

   Positive/negative indicates under/over planned cost for work performed.

2. Cost variance percentage

   $$\mathbf{CV\% = \frac{CV}{BCWP} \times 100}$$

3. Cost performance index

   $$\mathbf{CPI = \frac{BCWP}{ACWP}}$$

   Indicates whether work accomplished so far has been completed within budget. Over/under 1.0 indicates greater/lesser efficiency.

4. Schedule variance

   SV = BCWP – BCWS

   Positive/negative indicates ahead/behind planned schedule.

5. Schedule variance percentage

   $$\mathbf{SV\% = \frac{SV}{BCWS} \times 100}$$

6. Schedule performance index

   $$\mathbf{SPI = \frac{BCWP}{BCWS}}$$

   Indicates whether work accomplished so far has been achieved to schedule. Over/
   under 1.0 indicates greater/lesser than schedule achievement.

7. Schedule variance in months

   $$\mathbf{SV\ (mths) = \frac{SV\ (cum)}{Average\ Monthly\ BCWP}}$$

53

D.2   INDEPENDENT STATISTICAL FORECAST FORMULAE

1. Estimate at completion

$$EAC = ACWP + ETC$$

Extrapolations of future cost assuming past performance include:

2. Independent estimate to completion

$$ETC = \frac{(BAC - BCWP)}{CPI}$$

3. Independent estimate at completion

$$EAC = ACWP + \frac{BAC - BCWP}{CPI \times SPI}$$

4. To complete performance index for planned budget

$$TCPI\ (BAC) = \frac{BAC - BCWP}{BAC - ACWP}$$

To calculate the future cost performance index required to meet the planned budget.

5. To complete performance index for estimated out-turn costs

$$TCPI\ (EAC) = \frac{BAC - BCWP}{EAC - ACWP}$$

To calculate the future cost performance index required to meet the estimated out-turn costs.

D.3   OTHER FORMULAE

1. Percentage spent

$$\%\ Spent = \frac{ACWP}{BAC} \times 100$$

2. Percentage complete

$$\%\ Compt = \frac{BCWP}{BAC} \times 100$$

3. Variance at completion

$$VAC = BAC - EAC$$

4. Variance at completion percentage

$$VAC\ \% = \frac{VAC}{BAC} \times 100$$

INDEX